MY SECRET LIFE

Krisztina Tóth (*b.* 1967) is one of the most popular and best known Central European authors, and the recipient of numerous awards. She studied sculpting and literature in Budapest, spending two years in Paris during her university years. She has published nine books of poetry and ten books of prose to date as well as 24 books for children. In 2015, her novel *Aquarium* featured on the shortlist of the German Internationaler Literaturpreis. Her work has been translated into 25 languages; her novels, short stories and poems can be read in German, French, English, Polish, Finnish, Swedish, Czech and Spanish, among others. Her bestselling short novel *The Monkey's Eyes* was published in Hungary in 2023; an English translation is forthcoming from Seven Stories Press in the US.

Her children's books treat topics considered unusual, even taboo, in children's literature. *Mum Had an Operation* explains cancer to schoolchildren in a humorous and lyrical tone, while the main characters in *A Story for Nose-Blowers* are two members of the 'Snot family' who live in the right and the left cavity of a nose. *The Girl Who Wouldn't Talk* was inspired by the story of her own adopted daughter. Her musical *Wanderer of the Years* explains passing and letting go to children, while *Pokémon Go* and *The Rubber Bat* are for adults.

Her plays include *The Bat*, published in English translation in the compilation *Plays from Contemporary Hungary: 'Difficult Women' and Resistant Dramatic Voices* (Bloomsbury, 2023). Two collections of her short stories have also been published in English translation, *Pixel* (Seagull Books, 2019) and *Barcode* (Jantar Publishing, 2023). Her work was featured in George Szirtes' anthology *New Order: Hungarian Poets of the Post 1989 Generation* (Arc Publications, 2010). The first edition of her poetry in English, *My Secret Life: Selected Poems*, translated by George Szirtes, was published by Bloodaxe Books in 2025.

Krisztina Tóth

MY SECRET LIFE

SELECTED POEMS

translated from the Hungarian by
GEORGE SZIRTES

BLOODAXE BOOKS

Poems copyright © Krisztina Tóth 2001, 2004, 2009, 2016, 2021, 2025
Translations & introduction © George Szirtes 2025

ISBN: 978 1 78037 703 2

First published in the UK in 2025 by

Bloodaxe Books Ltd,

Eastburn,

South Park,

Hexham,

Northumberland NE46 1BS

www.bloodaxebooks.com
For further information about Bloodaxe titles
please visit our website and join our mailing list
or write to the above address for a catalogue.

This book has been selected to receive financial assistance from English
PEN's PEN Translates programme, supported by Arts Council England.
English PEN exists to promote literature and our understanding of it,
to uphold writers' freedoms around the world, to campaign against the
persecution and imprisonment of writers for stating their views, and to
promote the friendly co-operation of writers and the free exchange of ideas.
www.englishpen.org

Cover design: Neil Astley & Pamela Robertson-Pearce.

Printed in Great Britain by Bell & Bain Limited, Glasgow, Scotland, on
acid-free paper sourced from mills with FSC chain of custody certification.

ACKNOWLEDGEMENTS

This book presents a selection of her poems made by Krisztina Tóth for George Szirtes to translate, taken from five collections published by Magvető Kiadó in Budapest: *Porhó* (Dust, 2001), *Síró ponyva* (Weeping awning, 2004), *Magas labda* (High ball, 2009), *Világadapter* (Universal adaptor, 2016) and *Bálnadal* (Whalesong, 2021). The poems 'Homeward', 'Dodó' and 'Oven Glove' are previously unpublished in Hungarian in book form. In the contents list the initials [P], SP], [V], [ML] and [B] – or [U] for uncollected – indicate which of these collections each poem comes from.

CONTENTS

INTRODUCTION

The problem with writing an introduction to Krisztina Tóth's poetry is that there is so much more of her, of such variety and weight, and yet it all forms a coherent and dramatically persuasive whole. The voice in the poems is no different from the voice in the prose. They work slightly differently in terms of technique and scale – the prose perhaps more structurally experimental – but they are extensions of each other in terms of sensibility and vision.

There remains the issue of sheer variety and productivity. Tóth began as a poet and has written nine books of poetry, ten books of prose including novels and collections of short stories, and over twenty books for children as well as a couple of stage plays. She has worked with stained glass, translated French poetry, curated exhibitions, won numerous top honours, Hungarian and otherwise, and been translated into at least eighteen languages. But despite being a leading Hungarian writer with an international reputation, she is no longer able to live in Hungary under the new repressive climate fostered by the government of Viktor Orbán. I will return to this later.

Born in 1967, she is precisely of the generation I was hoping to explore in my anthology, *New Order: Hungarian Poets of the Post 1989 Generation* (Arc Publications, 2010), in which she was one of the twelve poets featured. This was the generation coming to maturity in the last years of what became known as 'goulash communism' – the old order – their first books appearing in or just after the revolutionary changes of 1989, the year Tóth's own first prizewinning book of poems appeared.

The breakthrough, the sense of liberation and possibility, the casting-off of powers and conditions that bred companionship in opposition before 1989, was quickly succeeded by the bleak reality of dramatic economic and political adjustment. Unemployment, homelessness, chaos, exploitation of chaos and, on a personal psychological level, a new kind of disillusion and alienation, not just from structures but from relationships, bred a new climate. People who had been friends in opposition stopped speaking to each other within months of the change.

It would be a grave mistake to project the embodiment of a social or political crisis on to specific individuals, especially writers, and perhaps most of all, poets. Poets are not sociologists. They respond to the extra-ordinary complexities of their lives and the lives around them in all the various instinctive dimensions open to each one of them individually.

Similarly with Krisztina Tóth who is a wonderful writer of poems of loss, helplessness, fury, and desire, as well as of social observation and a profound and moving understanding of mortality. She approaches such things with humour and with a clear sense of the tension between the fragility of form and the fragility of the physical world, but that world is clouded.

*

The voice in Tóth's poems is conversational, perfectly plain, but precise. It is almost always in the first-person singular. Usually, she is addressing us as a close friend that she trusts with certain confidences and the poems often hit us in mid-narrative, an untold story having been assumed. It is there we pick up. The experiences we encounter are ordinary enough but we sense movement under our feet.

> We were crossing the bridge. It's been like this a while, you said.
> I feel much the same, I said. We carried on walking.
> We stared straight ahead like people in a hurry.
> A tram ran past us and the pavement was juddering.

So begins the poem, 'Barrier'. Nothing is quite stable and even when it appears to be so, there is little to feel stable about. There are ended affairs, moments in affairs that hint at ends to come, there are desertions and the common everyday horrors of life at base level. It is a matter of cheap flats, cheap shopping, blocked toilets, second hand goods, a kind of kitchen-sink realism, or that at least is the setting and occasion.

Yet life holds together, or rather it rhymes, as she tells her class in 'The Student'

> Everything rhymes! – I keep repeating,
> the world is a fine web of sound,
> alert in every single strand,
> and your task is to be the spider!

And she gives examples:

> Yesterday, getting in the bath, I tell them,
> I spotted a dead cranefly on the floor,
> and, on the pavement, an umbrella inside out,
> a belated rhyme: both dead and drenched.

The spider hangs life together with the finest of threads. It is in these threads the poetry is fully alive. Sometimes it is rhyme itself as in 'Fig Tree':

> Late summer figs, their peak long past,
> are gently rotting underfoot.
> Wasps hovering in yellow grass
> strip away what's left of fruit.
>
> An old man rises from his bath
> his testicles hang low and soft.
> Branches requiring firm support
> panic and thrust their arms aloft.
>
> Ancient matron, skin like horn,
> recalls the children she once bore.
> The tree remembers weeping milk,
> her wrinkled breast is full once more…

The breast full once again is as far she gets to an image of redemption. The world the poems inhabit is unlikely to offer much redemption, but it does offer consolation. And there's memory:

> At a relative's house, back in my childhood,
> among the clumsy furniture, in the crowded flat
> of a widowed forester wearing a flannel shirt,
> there towered a vertical clock with a door

you could open. It was full of mechanical parts
that made it look mysterious yet pointless
like the empty dovecote in the courtyard
of a block where some of my school friends lived.
It's an upright clock, the adults earnestly told me
and since it had not worked for years, I felt
it must owe its dignity to its unmoving hands.

('Time, time, time')

Then there is love with its regrets and missed occasions, as in 'Tourist':

It was evening when I arrived in the town
you did not visit with me. People were going home:
women with closed faces, men with well-brushed hair.
It was glaringly obvious I was a stranger, so tired
I was dead on my feet.
I slept in a double bed
but they only laid out a single piece of chocolate.
The person at reception
suggested I use the safe in the cupboard.
I wondered what I might put there,
a souvenir perhaps, something
one couldn't lock, something expensive,
and how to manage life from then on
so I could forget the code
as soon as possible.

The world may be bereft of joy but it has its humour:

No pain? Are you paying attention at all?
No I wasn't. I was watching the light on the couch,
the way it shone through coloured rings
as in a church, like yellow, blue and red
leaded glass: I'd not seen that in a flat before.
He had to hurry, his mum was due at five.
His pants round his feet, he leapt after me
as I squatted in the bath and he stood at the tap.
I think it's great too. At its best in the morning.

And, in 'Ode to Men of Fifty':

> Where are you now, dear romantic boys,
> and where now, where indeed, your typewriters,
> their keys clogged with dandruff and wisps of hair –
> in what darkness do your hearts still judder
> wondering if this booming silence is the end of the matter
> or merely halfway there?
> I checked the size of my ass
> in the mirror, and well, it's not what it was,
> yet I fervently desire you, whoever you are,
> you and you alone

But desire has its sinister side as when, in 'Gumtree', she is ordering a doll online for her daughter and finds herself confronted with advertisements for inflatable sex-toys instead:

> I bid for it but was outbid by someone
> who wanted a little girl with a terrified face,
> a four-foot-three high silicone woman
> wearing knee-socks and sandals.
>
> There was, said the advertisement, a choice
> of three colours for hair and more for the eyes,
> with three welcome accommodating slits,
> vagina length six inches, fluids provided.

As one might guess there is a powerful feminist instinct at play, one that can locate its fury in the comfortable, handsome and exploitative patriarch in 'Lover's Dream'.

> My task there was to carry a parasol
> round the garden. The children too were my affair.
> Day and night I loved nothing better than to haul
> myself up and down those brilliant white stairs.
>
> There was a heavy shower and I grabbed the toys and took
> the little cushions to the terrace to keep them under cover,
> when, like someone reading an endless meaningless book,
> I realised that nothing here was useful or could be ever.

So then I cut their heads off and arranged them all
carefully in clean bottles with faces to the front
on either side of the marble steps, remaining vigilant
in case the blood should spill on the stairs or on the wall.

Where do her poems begin? What is their true base? She tells us in 'Where', a short poem that builds up a set of landscapes where a poem might begin as preparation for this conclusion:

…it doesn't begin there

but at the edge of the forest, in rotting humus
where somebody once was buried alive,
that's where the poem begins.

In 'My Secret Life', she tells us:

My secret life is lived at the edge of your widening cornea, discreetly,
close the lids of your scratched eyes on me, close them completely

Her most powerful, most universal vision is in the longer poem, 'Sleeper', which begins:

Where have you been, Sleeper, tell us about the server
that transmits such shaky images across the foggy water,
were you a seagull, did the precarious dream of
clinging to a mast seek you on some guano-covered cliff,
and were you dizzy, as you never had been before
so you saw how it was no use, that earth was no more
than the slippery minute, a cloakroom of woods and bodies,
a roar in a colonnade you must cross fully awake however unsteady
the way, could you see it as from above, a gorge compounded
of a single cry, tell us, Sleeper, what is it that is suspended
above the mountain, under the breathing sky and how light moves

Tóth is, and has been for several years, a major figure in Hungarian writing and, being a major figure with an important public voice, she has also been, and is now, subject to unrelenting attacks by the government-funded, government-supporting, gutter press.

Her books are still published in Hungary, but she has recently had to leave the country with her family. Originally attacked for suggesting that a couple of standard pieces of literature might be removed from the school syllabus and replaced with work by contemporary women writers, her life has become the subject of the sort of storm of defamation already practised on others perceived to be threatening the values of the government.

How does this work? A smear-piece appears in a newspaper. The name of its author is quickly removed but by then hundreds, maybe thousands of newspapers, national and local, as well as radio and television, have run with it. The victim receives anonymous death threats, excrement is pushed through her letterbox, gullible people in the street stop to curse at her. She becomes the object of daily hate. This level of persecution is easily triggered in a country where the government effectively commands all major forms of communication.

And it is not just the victim herself who suffers. Tóth and her previous husband adopted an abandoned Roma girl. The girl too has been abused to the edge of breakdown.

Although her current husband is British and would be very happy to bring the girl to England so she can be with her mother, the post-Brexit rule is that if one parent is resident elsewhere the UK authorities do not allow the child to live with the other parent in Britain. That is why Tóth and her family will be on the move again.

Under the private disappointments and alienation of the first-person speaker in Tóth's poems there is, as in 'Where', a deeper, more vicious set of circumstances.

Tóth's poems are not about the concerns of one person. They – as well her stories and novels – are about pity in remorseless places. They are essentially a form of tragic writing conducted through irony, with precision, with formal distance, and a discipline as remorseless as the conditions it faces.

GEORGE SZIRTES

East European Triptych

I

We spring to our feet when they call our names
on the loudspeaker. Our names
are misspelt and mispronounced,
but we smile enthusiastically.
We're carrying soap from hotels,
we leave too early for the station.
Our fellow nationals are all over the place
with heavy cases, wearing baggy trousers.
We get on the wrong trains, and if we pay,
our loose change simply rolls away.

We are scared even at our own border
and are lost once past it, but we recognise
each other. Even on the far side of the world
we know each other by our sweat drenched clothes.
The moving stairs stop under us, our full
shopping bags break off at the handles and when
we leave, the alarm siren goes off.
Under our skins, like a precious jewel,
glows the microchip of guilt.

II

I know where you live. I'm familiar with the city.
I'm familiar too with the black rain.
Your mother would lie and sunbathe on the roof,
in summer you'd swim in the gravel pit.
I remember people who'd lost their legs
who made their home in shelters in doorways.

I'm familiar with the country, I have known
its trains, its weeping, its chlorine-coloured sky,
its acid rain, its long slow fall of snow,
its overdressed, pale babies.

I know where you live but whatever you do,
whenever you think of home, your dreams
are full of avenues lined by stunted acacias.
After Christmas when others are dragging the tree
by its feet like an overweight corpse,
you stop and watch them dumping it with the rest.
I know what you see. A tangled pile of human bodies
their yellow arms extended, wearing forgotten
blue and gold sweet wrappers like stolen jewellery.

III

My name is Alina Moldova.
I come from East Europe,
I am 170 centimetres tall,
my life expectancy is 56 years.
My mouth is full of amalgam fillings,
my heart full of inherited anxieties.
No one understands when I speak English
nor when I try to speak French,
the only language I speak without accent
is the language of fear.

My name is Alina Moldova,
my heart valve is an unmanned level crossing,
my veins are full of circulating poisons,
my life expectancy is 56 years.
I can manage my ten-year-old boy,
I find some flour, I leap on a moving train.

You can hit me, you can shake me about,
only my earrings will rattle
like a long-defunct component
in an engine that's still running.

Sleeper

Where have you been, Sleeper, tell us about the server
that transmits such shaky images across the foggy water,
were you a seagull, did the precarious dream of
clinging to a mast seek you on some guano-covered cliff,
and were you dizzy, as you never had been before
so you saw how it was no use, that earth was no more
than the slippery minute, a cloakroom of woods and bodies,
a roar in a colonnade you must cross fully awake however unsteady
the way, could you see it as from above, a gorge compounded
of a single cry, tell us, Sleeper, what is it that is suspended
above the mountain, under the breathing sky and how light moves
through the huge pink cloud of the lungs, how the cuts and grooves
of the mouth gurgle with foam and how the stalactite
of the uvula sparkles in the dripping valley of the throat,
and further still what images are etched by salt, lime and ice,
how earth is just a folded map, how God stares into the pit of the eye,
tell us what water says and what is slopping in the ranks of waves,
what are the creatures buzzing, and does it hurt when they weave
and change shape, when naked gooseflesh under fur gone cold
and dropped feathers throbs, screams, quivers and is called
by name, where have you been Sleeper, recount your flimsy,
whirlpool dreams of oil-slicked seas and seventeen tons of greasy
hair, tell us of wounds still smoking on earth scarred with fire,
give us aerial views of bridges like white stitches and of tight
twists of fate, the intricate fingerprints of winding highways
on a well-thumbed world as you swim past the breakwater of estates,
show us, Sleeper, the shadow island of fishes and large ships
and how the dead set out in search of other forms of life for fellowship,
how the tides of the sky rock the buoys of the stars, how they all fall away,
how vapour is ground down to breath, and how the blue light sways
on creaking chains and twilight, then swims on, its heavy metal seeping

into mud, and tell us of the corridors you passed through while sleeping,
how many vast spaces you crossed, and how the secret moment becomes
a door and what it's like to step into such cold, unlit fiefdoms,
does anything remain, do you recall the foam of your life, think back,
do you carry your fate like the slow flow of the corpse in a sack,
does the noisy past roll past you on its carpet in your occasional presence
or are you talking to the ocean through a thousand years of silence,
repeating what the radar of your brief life enabled you to witness
tell us little pulse box, will the soul sink into depths above us
or will it spin and billow like a bladder of light, understanding nothing,
blind, transparent, a never decomposing, murderous thing,
an empty flask of pills, doomed to roam the sky's thin covering?

River of Sounds

The heart under the heart throbs on, word bubbles under sound,
     sentence under sentence whirlpools under the bridge:
What does the deep river in spate continue to swirl round,
     and what does its wrinkled bed carry on the sludge?
Time and again bodies come floating down the flood
     that prints the electric circuit of cities on the night,
houses with algae facades, streetlamps crumbling into mud
     emerge from the dark like memories of flight.
It murmurs names and explores meandering routes
     to sloping gardens and palaces on the coast,
past waterlogged villages and men in muddied boots,
     its dreams stuffed with mouldy canvas and damp ghosts.
It speaks of melon-rinds, silence on water-stained walls,
     of rooms where maps of time are drawn, continually
repeating themselves, scrolling sentences in a dying fall,
     and of wide bays where wrecks congregate and eddy,
scrolling images of wavering moons in its looking glass
     with shape-shifting time while the sky is a pulse,
a gateway through which signs, like the dead, must pass,
     where everything is quotation, a pool for something else,
and in all that flow of words there must be a place
     where heart beats beneath heart to the drone of apprehensions,
the whirlpool of funnels, the river of resounding voices.

    II

Who is that prattling on, wave on wave, like the tide
     like an army of sleepwalkers with a wild look in their eyes?
Her eyes, her eyes, if only I could recall them opened wide,
     but she was asleep, with her back to me, white and cold as ice,
and you did not love me mother, so what was that about,

what drifts in the deep river, Mother, *Anya* with a capital A,
what happened that night when you left me there to float,
 the narrative weeps and washes itself away,
one day I got lost, all streets were the same,
 no yellow house, no butchers shop, my bike too
vanished, only my father shouldn't catch on to the game,
 then suddenly evening, with war news coming through,
fat children's hands, men's clipped fingernails,
 women's hands washing plastic dishes, an endless
fence, fruit dropped on concrete, thunder approaching, gales,
 come on now, I've been looking for you for ages,
a blue bike lies on the ground by the boathouse
 what did you see down there, a rusty lid, a heap
of cash, the earth is a gateway of signs, it makes figures,
 grows old, obliterating dried-up roads that time strips
to the bone century by century, there must be a place, by the river
 of words, a dumping ground, a secret place, where drowned
things gather in piles, a place with a name that is never pronounced.

III

Human speech bubbles past, children are crying in the sun
 branch of a poplar tree on the embankment,
parents whisper conversations in the early dawn
 gabble-talk between stones, dead leaves spread
on waves, memories like light off a fish's back,
 dead cats hitting the banks, backs against the flow,
shapeless clothes, broken wicker baskets, a green bough slack
 with leaves, a paper bag flapping there and letting go,
the strengthening current spins empty bottles where they float
 and drags unfortunates into the gritty mud
so only traces remain, and, after tears, the taste of salt,
 a scattering of debris, anonymous faces on the flood,
behind closed eyes clouds jostle, translucent shoals

of fish press towards the mouth of the heart
like a stray arrow shot into blue air, and a swirl of gulls
        crying in the wind in a ring then blown apart,
pages of soaked books, bodies of mice, dead weight,
        decomposing quilts in decaying bundles of feathers
borne on the wave, sinking, the noise of the inchoate,
        open eyed days lost under the tongue forever,
voices drumming under voices, a drench of word on word,
        unnamed waterfalls that speak of embankments in bloom,
a deep arterial road, blind corridors, an unheard
        curtain of water opening on countless shadow rooms.

Lover's Dream

I applied as palace guard, the people were beautiful
just as he was himself, his children blond and lithe.
The house was on a hillside down a shady avenue.
They waved to me from the gate, all bonny and blithe.

Their dog was my dog once. I took them a drawing
to show them as she once was. I liked them: they liked me.
We got to planning how we could live there together
in peace and happiness the colour of weak tea.

The wife was blind, scrubbing the white stairs.
He pointed her out to me and said, that is my wife.
He was all tenderness as he bent down to her,
and I waited for him to escort me to the roof.

My task there was to carry a parasol
round the garden. The children too were my affair.
Day and night I loved nothing better than to haul
myself up and down those brilliant white stairs.

There was a heavy shower and I grabbed the toys and took
the little cushions to the terrace to keep them under cover,
when, like someone reading an endless meaningless book,
I realised that nothing here was useful or could be ever.

So then I cut their heads off and arranged them all
carefully in clean bottles with faces to the front
on either side of the marble steps, remaining vigilant
in case the blood should spill on the stairs or on the wall.

I shed some tears but I knew I wasn't crazy,
since it was his gaze that triggered it somehow,
and I felt sorry that I would never again see
that solemn, perspiring and very handsome brow.

Tyrannosaurus Rex

I remember nothing of Maribor,
nothing that I should remember.
All I know I have learned from others:
I don't remember those three days.

I remember nothing of Ljubljana either
only that you promised you would come.
Ljubljana is just a hotel to me.
Ljubljana means simply: you're not there.

I remember nothing of the mountains
but everyone waiting on the bus for me.
I was busily counting up my cash
because I had spotted a dinosaur backpack.

I bought it for my son but had no room for it.
I ran because the driver was sounding his horn.
For a whole week I carried that backpack
up and down Slovenian mountains.

Those who saw me will remember only
a woman, possibly Polish, maybe Hungarian,
who carried her luggage in a dinosaur backpack
and never once spoke to anyone that week.

It turned out, at the beginning of the term,
that dinosaur backpacks were immensely popular
though it should be said that, among backpacks,
Tyrannosaurus Rex was the rarest and the largest.

Emperor of lizards, insatiable carnivore,
you were not slow in gobbling up my days.
Somebody, one time, mentioned Ljubljana
and that the name derives from 'city of love'.

I waited for you a whole six million years
but only once did we speak to each other after.
Such deep dull hurt is doomed to meet its sad
demise, the way the dinosaurs met theirs.

Tourist

It was evening when I arrived in the town
you did not visit with me. People were going home:
women with closed faces, men with well-brushed hair.
It was glaringly obvious I was a stranger, so tired
I was dead on my feet.
I slept in a double bed
but they only laid out a single piece of chocolate.
The person at reception
suggested I use the safe in the cupboard.
I wondered what I might put there,
a souvenir perhaps, something
one couldn't lock, something expensive,
and how to manage life from then on
so I could forget the code
as soon as possible.

The town you didn't visit with me
was colder than at home. The streets were windy
and I spent hours gazing at shop windows.
I spent a whole hour
in a Chinese shop, the assistant eying me
suspiciously from behind the till.
It was glaringly obvious
that I was a stranger
and dead on my feet.
How fragile we are
Sting was crooning on the radio,
so I went to pay, fiddling with small change.
The toy robot that looked fine in the luggage
went wrong the minute we took it out.
It span and span then fell flat on its back

and stared straight up from the carpet,
as if – said my son, examining the battery –
someone had plucked its heart out.

But even when you did come things went wrong.
Once, in another town, you woke
with a scab in your mouth and we couldn't
think of the English for herpes.
You pursed your lips and pointed at your mouth
like a cheap Romeo as you leaned across the counter.
The woman in the lab coat looked at you in disgust
till she finally understood what you meant.
In yet another town the toilet was blocked
and we stared at the bowl in the rented apartment,
the turd like the tip of a frightened animal's tail.
It gurgled when we tried to flush it down the pan
and we were too scared to mess around with it.
The Portuguese plumber asked where we were from
and if we were used to modern appliances
such as flushing toilets and cisterns with handles.
When they're not mocking you, they're gypping you,
– you remarked in bed later. We spent the night
talking about workmen rather than making love.

Pretty soon I had walked every street of the town
you did not visit with me. The ornamental clock
in the main square counted the hours not spent with you.
A man with a laptop kept staring at me,
the scent of his after-shave filling the lift.
I felt I could love anybody then,
anyone except you. I could walk round town with him
while he awkwardly carried his umbrella
and I could lie that you were calling me from home
though it was just a message about my balance.

By now I was out of everything,
out of weary old arguments,
out of ill-fitting clothes and my ill-fitted life.
It was glaringly obvious that I was a stranger
and dead on my feet.
I kept pressing the wrong button on the coffee machine
and when I backed off, the steam kept spouting,
and there wasn't a clean table anywhere.

The town you didn't visit with me
was pummelled by rain. It took me
three years to return.
The rain had grown since then.
Cutting a path between transparent shoots of it
with my umbrella, I found my way back to the shop.
The goods on offer had hardly changed.
I bought a new purse and threw the old one,
the one I had when we were still together
into a bin in the hotel car park. No one
saw me but I still felt like
a cheat, a pickpocket who, having robbed
someone not mentioned in this poem,
was wheeling her baggage away
leaving the bill for her unpaid past behind.

I hold that town responsible, the town you didn't
visit with me, the town where missing objects go.
How many such towns have I visited since!
It is you that I have to thank for having become
a professional tourist, someone who keeps crossing borders
never forgetting that wherever she is
she has to go home some time.
Till then I'll make do with a decent map
so I can go anywhere, wandering down

the crowded alleys of memory,
recalling whole continents of a previous life
and a long-buried bathroom where
it still lingers like an angry old punk,
its face turned to the tiles,
its white bristles stiff with dry paste,
your stupid electric toothbrush

Send Me a Smile

I saw your eyes on the Metro in a stranger's face.
There are days when everything reminds me of something else.
I spot somebody or other and you have taken their place.
This is the second successive year playing me false.

An old school friend walks up in the same childhood frame.
Frankly I never believed that that could happen to us.
Lord only knows how much I wanted it to be the same.
Then there you are on the Metro, suddenly older, more cavernous.

I used to wonder what our two bodies might say to the other's call,
What you would smell like, quite different now no doubt.
Could our two bodies speak to each other at all?
There is a faint scar where my son pushed his way out.

I don't know what to make of the widening of my hips.
I'm neither pleased nor exhausted by the fact.
It was strange gazing at another's eyes and lips.
You with your alien eyes seeing my lips react.

*

Sometimes when I speak, I'm shocked to hear my mother.
Last time she addressed me in a mirror at the movies.
It was the way she held the soap that got me in a bother.
All those years of shit back then, what good did they do me?

And the man I live with now, I get it with him too.
And something about my dog and the look in his eyes.
I'm not lying about my mother. Why would I lie to you?
I don't know why I mention these things. I don't think it's wise.

It was the last Christmas of my childhood. They gave me a kitten.
We lived next to a grocer. It was snowing. A busy road.
She saw me and dashed across to me. I've not forgotten.
It's the same old lesson you take on, load by load.

Before it hardens a chestnut is a leaf on a tree.
That's right, you'd answer, in so many words.
Yes, I've seen that happen and it could be me.
Crazy, I say, to think I'm one of nature's nerds.

*

We moved into the house in early fall last year.
Everything was thick dust and thin paint.
We wondered if by breathing we could change the smell in there.
Then it grew cooler but the memory grows faint.

Suddenly you couldn't spend morning on the terrace.
You took your coffee out. It was cold even in a coat.
There was nothing left to occupy, there was no space.
But one adapts and reinvents, one stays afloat.

The light's so strange today it's like a far-off season.
I'm somebody else today or simply elsewhere.
I go in for a cardigan but it's still freezing.
It's not the colours but the texture of the air.

It's not summer but fall that's on the go.
A patch of rust like a silent mouth, the face of a leaf.
A cat with baby eyes: my son's look years ago.
The wind drops. I keep watching as the thin smoke drifts.

Dog

It seemed no more than a clump of earth in the thaw,
a snowball that had rolled down a steep slope.
The day was darkening, nothing to see at all
just fields like tin, the windscreen part steamed up,
but as we neared it seemed vaguely to shift
like a heavy coat raising a loose sleeve,
a ditched hitchhiker's shade thumbing a lift
in the brief glare that passing headlights weave.
It was there one moment, gone the next. Each car
in the queue steered well clear of the thing
but I looked out for it on the hard verge
and suddenly there it was. It was propping
itself up on its legs, the nearside ones in sludge
as if about to run, its nose held to the air,
its upper part attent. But behind I saw
its lower half, wrecked to a pulp. And there,
from its blood-clotted coat, stuck its back leg
that to a regular, agonising pulse kept kicking;
mouth wide open, it sat there, a half-dog
though I could tell from its eyes that it saw everything.
I cried out, Stop! draw up at the side
of the road. I begged you to save it or kill it now,
anything, let the cars behind us provide
an ending. But what can I do? What? Just how
should I end it? And so your voice grew sharp.
What do you want of me? What is it you want? Tell me!
I wanted you not to leave it, I wanted you to stop.
Once you found it you should look after it or kill it.
A week we tended the dog, because we thought
at least it's better off home with us giving it attention,
as if it were we ourselves who had hit it and left it out

in the road, a fact we had somehow not to mention.
But I could still not help wanting you wrapped
about me at night: I watched your muscular arm,
trying not to think of the body that lay propped
in the roadside ditch, of the leg beating like a drum
while your eyes were focused somewhere far away
but did not answer; about the constant fury
and resignation involved in even love-making, and the way
you asked me just what it was that I wanted you to do,
striking the steering wheel over and over again,
and not once looking directly at me, while I
watched as beyond your shoulder rain beat down,
soaking fields under the bloodshot winter sky.

Barrier

We were crossing the bridge. It's been like this a while, you said.
I feel much the same, I said. We carried on walking.
We stared straight ahead like people in a hurry.
A tram ran past us and the pavement was juddering.

The river was grey, the barges were gently rocking.
There were certain matters that couldn't be finalised.
A gull flew past and landed, a cyclist pedalled by.
A decade had passed, the embankment was deserted.

Against the changing backcloth of the billowing sky,
two figures drifted past as on a dream-scanner.
Another tram went by, my heart was juddering,
under the trembling bridge swirled the grey water.

New Year's Eve

So here's another year that I've sent packing.
It's leaving right now, all dressed up as snow.
I know you exist, that it is you I'm lacking
and that's OK since you're out there, I know,

in some imaginable solid place
or pretty close, lost to a different night,
though when I look there searching for your face
they're strangers all, and you're nowhere in sight,

and even I, when I unpack my bag
seem to be carrying other people's stuff:
handkerchiefs, keys, soaked identity tag,
would you know me by such things, is that enough?

Could you tell me by my shoes, the coat I wear?
In cloakrooms could you recognise the one
I carried and confidently declare
that it was mine before I put it on?

I see this very room as in a mirror:
as familiar yet strange, a spacious den,
a life I'd entered by some kind of error,
a night I should sleep off and start again

after a millennium of heavy sleep.
Let me forget you, may you sink so deep
that when they ask me for my name, may I
not answer with your name when I reply.

Folder

No pain? Are you paying attention at all?
No I wasn't. I was watching the light on the couch,
the way it shone through coloured rings
as in a church, like yellow, blue and red
leaded glass: I'd not seen that in a flat before.
He had to hurry, his mum was due at five.
His pants round his feet, he leapt after me
as I squatted in the bath and he stood at the tap.
I think it's great too. At its best in the morning.

I was sixteen. Sixteen years later
he was standing beside me on a red number 7:
…the leaded glass, you know, between the dining room
and the day room, you preserved that didn't you?
…of course not. My father did that. He stuck
coloured folders between two sheets of glass,
he brought them home from work…
…I'm getting off, I change to the Metro here.

Why does everything wonderful no longer glow?
Father Christmas. The stork. And now this.

Ode to Men of Fifty

Where are you now, dear romantic boys,
and where now, where indeed, your typewriters,
their keys clogged with dandruff and wisps of hair –
in what darkness do your hearts still judder
wondering if this booming silence is the end of the matter
or merely halfway there?
I checked the size of my ass
in the mirror, and well, it's not what it was,
yet I fervently desire you, whoever you are,
you and you alone,
my darlings of forty going on
fifty, with your backache
and your hair greying as expected
your smile displaying
its rotting canines,
your hands trembling
like your voice on the phone.
But you go on living in all those ugly
tiepins in my pin-pricked life,
in every airless love affair,
in every flat and stairwell,
in your full gamut of smells.
A fifty-year old man is like
a poplar bough, fallen in the street,
fit for the fire, slow to light, that burns with a blue flame,
but willing now and then to shimmer in the autumn bonfire,
present even when invisible,
like the air down in a mine, as in a dream.

Gumtree

I was looking for a doll, a small children's doll
to replace the old one my daughter had lost,
a doll as much like the first one as possible.
It would make her a present at Christmas.

I wrote that it should be a second-hand item
but one in perfect condition, hoping
that among so many I would find one exactly
like the first and dress it in new clothes.

The site popped up with a body, one bigger
by far than a baby should ever be, that stared
back at me like a ghost from the past,
begging me please to take her away with me.

But good heavens, what is this I see?
This is not what I want, no, not this baby,
this tortured creature in a foetal position,
but this was what the screen is showing me.

I bid for it but was outbid by someone
who wanted a little girl with a terrified face,
a four-foot-three high silicone woman
wearing knee-socks and sandals.

There was, said the advertisement, a choice
of three colours for hair and more for the eyes,
with three welcome accommodating slits,
vagina length six inches, fluids provided.

The fluids were intended for cleaning.
Someone out there had already paid the price,
and it had been sent out, so it would have a daddy.
Packing discreet, delivered by messenger.

I would have liked to take the body away
so I could give it a decent burial
in the longish box provided, before
the ground froze hard in winter.

A cardboard coffin containing childhood.
I would have scraped some soil over it
so something within it should find rest at last,
but the price was too high. It was too much to pay.

There's always a face somewhere
that reminds us of another, a lost face,
but when I call to it, it sinks under the surface
and starts crying again whenever I look for it.

There's always some minor detail missing from it.
How often did I hear my father tell me, you'll never
be satisfied, not even God's wallet is enough for you.
But where is God now? And how much is enough?

Where

Not there, on the tight bend of the paved highway,
where cars are occasionally prone to skidding,
chiefly in winter, though no one dies there,

not there where streets are greener and leafier
where lawns are mowed and there's a dog in the garden
and the head of the family gets home late at night,

nor there in front of the school where every morning
a man is waiting regular as clockwork,
nor inside the gates on the concrete playground,

nor in the neglected, dehydrated meadow
where a discarded dog-end hits the ground and glows
for a moment, it doesn't begin there

but at the edge of the forest, in rotting humus
where somebody once was buried alive,
that's where the poem begins.

Valley Road

I went out running carrying two stones,
one in either hand, because
last time on the downward slope
dogs started following me.

The road was clear now.
The valleys had darkened.
Fields of wheat were caving
under the slant light.

I was wondering as I ran
how they ploughed the fields below
and how machines could cross
that pitted lunar landscape.

There was hardly any traffic now.
I opened my arms wide,
and held out the heavy stones
as if flying with weights.

I tried to see how long I could fly,
busily beating my wings.
I was moving like a child,
a few cars manoeuvred round me.

They didn't know what this woman
in the cap was doing here among the hills,
running like that, and seeming to wave
while holding something in her hands.

The village was way behind me now,
and dusk had grown deeper,
I looked ever smaller to myself
as I followed the ribbon of the road.

On one side the declining sun
combed through the trees,
and my shadow fell across
the gleaming concrete surface.

Suddenly it was very quiet.
My shadow was enormous,
a giant Lego figure embracing
the cooling air.

Song of the Secret Life

My secret life is that of a cat sneaking between parked cars,
a shadow on a wall, a memory, its hem ripped apart,

My secret life is lived at the edge of your widening cornea, discreetly,
close the lids of your scratched eyes on me, close them completely,

My secret life is an echoing empty room in my head
where I leant from the window once and sang of blackness and dread.

My secret life is a ramshackle pigeon-loft stinking of shit,
a pale frock in the sky into which death will eventually fit.

My secret life is a deep crack that runs down a living face,
a path under time where I no longer rage, a singular place.

My secret life is a station where a train thunders through it and then
nothing but silence, pitch darkness, while I count to ten.

My secret life consists of moments quickly scanned in,
a crumpled page from a lost notebook found in the bin

My secret life is a lacking, an utter mystery, a puzzle undone,
so you have to read all my fading faces as if they were one.

My secret life is landfill, yellow and overflowing,
the lusts of the body in movement, time spent coming and going.

My secret life is kept secret on purpose with doors I always lock,
where dreams come at dawn with their knuckles and loudly knock.

My secret life is this thing you see passing, you catch it neatly,
close the lids of your scratched eyes on me, close them completely,

My secret life is one I've invented, to survive it needs telling,
its lightbulbs burn in the house, in that far distant dwelling.

Universal Adaptor

In the rainy autumn of two-thousand and two,
more than ten years ago,
I was in Boots by Charing Cross Station
where I found a tiny white universal adaptor.
It cost £8.50 so I put it in my basket,
but then returned it because once I reached the till
I reflected on the cost and it seemed too expensive.
Instead I bought a light, bright-coloured
gold-embroidered scarf.

What happened to the scarf? The wind stripped it
of its thin gold threads as it does the cellophane
on a cigarette pack. No one wears that kind now
and it got left on a luggage rack or under a coat
on a coat-stand in some foreign place.
Looking back on it now it is obvious
that putting that small white handy universal adaptor
back on the shelf in Boots next to
Charing Cross Station was a bad decision.

For, good heavens, what, after all, is £8.50!
It is no more than £1.07 per continent,
that's all it costs for the whole world's house-trained
currents to zip along wires and into
your clever gizmo. It's only ever in retrospect
that you realise what you should have done,
it's like being in a strange town with a folded
street map, leaving your soul ever further behind,
with a coloured scarf around your neck.

The world in the meantime continues to pulse
through your body unnoticed, and might be
shut off any time, producing extra tension,
not to mention peaks and fluctuations.
One bad decision, one temptation overcome,
one reconsidered moment and whole years
are immediately wasted. By the time
I returned to London, the shop that had been
the occasion of my error was no longer there.

Or was it that I simply failed to find it?
I carefully examined every shop window
and while of course, there were plenty of scarves,
even on temporary street stalls,
hundreds just like the one I had before,
there was not one universal adaptor to be had
at either stations or airports and what they did have
was never like the one I had returned.

Now I watch people coming and going,
their faces ashen and lined, of no particular age,
and try to guess who, among all those travellers
might actually possess one, someone who knows
at a moment's notice, how to adapt the world
and its gizmos to the pounding of so many hearts,
who can pack the thing, winding away the lead,
and carry the clever little universal adaptor
safe in its slip-case without breaking it.

It might after all be possible, after so many years
to ask if the hotel would lend me one
or never again to travel,
not to require any kind of gizmo,

nor to buy the first one I come across,
and it might be OK even without a slipcase
since it's never too late to buy an adaptor
since I was young and the scarf was just right for me.

Time, time, time

(for Judit Scherter)

At a relative's house, back in my childhood,
among the clumsy furniture, in the crowded flat
of a widowed forester wearing a flannel shirt,
there towered a vertical clock with a door
you could open. It was full of mechanical parts
that made it look mysterious yet pointless
like the empty dovecote in the courtyard
of a block where some of my school friends lived.
It's an upright clock, the adults earnestly told me
and since it had not worked for years, I felt
it must owe its dignity to its unmoving hands.
My parents wore wristwatches but never had the time
so I began to pine for a distant realm elsewhere
where I would eventually get to own
an upright clock of my own whose hands
could not be touched by anyone else.

Don't hold us up, they demanded, whenever we set out.
One day I was bored. I was sitting on the floor,
leafing through a hunting manual, gazing
at images of wide-eyed rabbits and deer.
It's hard work holding up people. Years pass before
you learn to get inside and behind time's back.
I delay whatever I can in the shadows.
I drag dead time along, its feet tied closely together,
pulling it behind me like a sledge.
What is that string, they ask, and what's at the end of it?
What are you dangling over the horizon?
Nothing, I tell them. Other times they ask
who is actually doing the pulling.

It's me, I answer on such occasions,
me when I'm older.

Don't run out of time, they used to say to me,
or you won't get a degree, a house, or a child,
you'll miss the last bus, the love of your life,
you won't be a ballerina or a young mother
not even an old one, you can't simply run
through a crowd on bare feet the whole of your life,
just look at your feet, you are still wearing
those sandals from childhood, its straps are loose,
quickly now, hurry, catch up with the others!
I ran like a deer, like a rabbit, in different shoes,
in dream shoes, my eyes open wide,
my stomach retching, my ribs pounding,
always falling behind, always stumbling
towards a corner of the picture. When I looked up
it was dark already and my time was up.

How Are You All?

It's the way the unsuspecting seventh
generation of the family gives birth
to the lion-faced, skin-blotched infant,
the way the obscene graffiti still shows
through the freshly painted outside wall,
the way your shit- and piss-smelling half-
demented granny emerges from the outhouse
and sticks her finger into the soup bowl,
the way, behind that lethargic monkey-mask,
locked for eternity onto an alien body,
death flashes across your friend's face
in one stubborn, momentary, familiar expression.

Were you to turn round for another look
you'd find they were gone. Somebody
would have sent your granny home, the house
would have been repainted and the new born
carted off never to be mentioned again,
while the monkey simply scratches and shows you
its swollen buttocks. How are you, you'd ask
over the steady grumble of buses at the bend,
the hum of electric cables and the faint boom
of the tube train under your feet. And, ever louder,
you'd shout to each other how you must get together
until one of you, faced with that wall of noise,
eventually steals a glance at her watch.

Duration

Everyone's gone, that's what it says on the paper,
it's the poor line I have been reciting as mantra.
It is not a good line. I shouldn't have written it.
There's a scratchy sound. The electric clock is a nuisance.
It's never silent here. A neighbour is shouting on her cell phone,
using unfamiliar terms that don't fit the poem.
Completion, duration, functioning business plan.
I am waiting for him to finish the conversation.
Down in the street he is arguing about time
with a phantom, how it can't go on like this.
If she gave up now I'd be doing the same,
talking about time, here in this poem.
I stand and lean from the window so I can see her.
There was a storm last night and the street is still wet.
There's a phrase in my head but it can't get out.
Something unexpected has blown the circuit.

On the path by the house there's a tall unidentifiable
plant growing from under the bushes.
I leave it there and return to the bad line
but now that I've noticed the plant the thought of it
bothers me. *Duration.* Another hour wasted,
what is the phrase, good heavens, where will this end,
I stand up and walk down to the car park
to explore the plant that is in the bushes.
There I discover a Mermaid Barbie with a crushed head
its mermaid tail stuck in the ground. It's as if it were
trying to tell me that it's under some kind of curse
that I should be lifting so it can get back in the water.
What is it doing here? It must be the storm
that has blown it away, or someone dropped it last night.

I am standing in the car park, bending over
as the mud-caked Barbie's eyes stare back at me.

And now what to do, what should I do now,
am I ever going to get some silence here?
Maybe someone is watching me from upstairs?
What has this strange moment to do with me?
Should I pull the thing out of the ground so it
sheds earth every night, because however often
we wash it, or wrap it in a tissue or leave it
on the radiator we'll only have to bin it in the end?
Or should I leave it here, so it might grow a little
each night like a scary, blonde, mutant carrot,
shaking its mountain of hair across our fervid future
as if in revenge, casting sand even on years to come,
when I will always have to see it in front of me,
pushing me forward and down inviting me to share her fate?
I stand there in my slippers, my coat open
and everyone's gone, like the line says, everyone's gone.

Camera

Hundreds at a time, no sooner than hatched,
they drop to the conveyor belt while the machine
propels them forward at an even pace
to funnels through which new born chicks arrive
at a terminus of wire cells where lights
maintain them at a steady temperature.

Meanwhile the dead are quickly lifted out
by nimble multi fingered hands on metal wrists,
their fate to be ground down to a fine meal.
No corpse gets past the hands that pounce on it,
that hover above the belt like a snail's shell.
like the shadow of this one fateful day.

One scruffy individual in that haplessly
blinking scrum of fluff happens to look up
raising its small beaked face to the funnel
where it is fixed in a flash by God's blind gaze
beaming across the furthest reaches of space.
But then it vanishes straight down the funnel.

It is as if he had asked its creator if there
was any point to this, any kind or meaning,
and if there might be a nest or belt on the other side.
But their eyes never did meet. Perhaps it was just
that the revolving eye had turned away for a moment.

Twenty Lines with a Cat

From the door of the house opposite emerges
a woman in a tracksuit. Where is she going?
She tiptoes up the garden to the *thuyas*,
the tin bowl she carries almost overflowing.

I see the bowl quite clearly from up here,
the amber liquid in it looks alarming.
Is she some madwoman emptying her pee
at the bottom of the garden every morning?

Or maybe it's just soup that has gone wrong
and she doesn't want to block the drains with it.
There are always a lot of cats under the bushes
and one that's thirsty might well lap at it.

The woman stops, looks where to leave the dish.
It's water and rat poison in suspension
with a stock cube added to disguise the smell
and to distract the rats' attention.

Inventing this gains me a little time.
Decades or months perhaps, or just a day.
It's neither game, nor voodoo: it's decision.
The cats will drink the stuff in their sly way.

Hourglass

Among the small ads for furniture
you'll always find an offer of free beds.
They are dead men's beds, although the vendors
tend to claim they are simply moving house.

Which is not in fact a lie because the figure
twisting and turning on the uncomfortable
mattress of pain has really moved away
by exchanging one kind of bed for another.

With what embarrassed enthusiasm they show
the young couple without much money to spare
how firm the headboard and the iron frame,
and how the mattress just needs a new cover...

So the beds arrive in narrow, sub-let attics
secured to the roof-rack by elastic spiders,
ready to assume their new lives to prepare
fresh generations to be bred in them.

There's the bedside table with its yellow light bulb,
a different body's weight under the blanket.
It's like turning an hourglass upside down
to give the stage-hands time to change the set.

But the noise and apparatus is much the same,
more weeping, more switching on the lamp,
more nappy, cotton wool, cream and sponge,
nappy, cotton wool and cream.

Sunday

They'll do, my mother nudges me at the socks
with 'Sunday' written on them, I need ten pairs,
hurry, she insisted, it's almost twelve o'clock,
my husband can't eat, he just sleeps and lies there,
his legs are cold and he is barely breathing,
I made him chicken soup to keep him going.

They good socks, the Chinese shop girl said.
The fallen tower of him had collapsed, he was flat out,
a butterfly had settled on the delicately spread
petals of his veins, its stiff wings shut.
Good sock, repeated the shop-girl, bright-eyed
as she licked her fingers to open the bag wide.

She said nothing, of course, about the leeching dye,
poor fabric, and the stitches coming loose,
they were good socks, she said, nodding away
as she helped me empty a sack ready for use.
The socks, as it happened, stayed in the hospital
and as to what day it was I've no idea at all.

My inheritance: this ball in a nylon bag.
Do you remember, dad, the moment at the fair
when, wonder of wonders, I took that ball of rag
and toppled the tower of cans erected there.
With rag balls in your hand you whispered, Wow!
How do you do that, was that sheer luck just now?

Since then I've tried, however long it took,
to repeat that one-off triumph, to take aim
and topple the tower once more as by a fluke.

You look down but I fail, each time the same.
Sunday, Sunday, that autumn afternoon,
I'm freezing here and it will be dark soon.

Fig Tree

Late summer figs, their peak long past,
are gently rotting underfoot.
Wasps hovering in yellow grass
strip away what's left of fruit.

An old man rises from his bath
his testicles hang low and soft.
Branches requiring firm support
panic and thrust their arms aloft.

Ancient matron, skin like horn,
recalls the children she once bore.
The tree remembers weeping milk
her wrinkled breast is full once more.

New owners walk the garden lawn
treading fruit already split,
theirs is the future they have crushed,
each fig a womblike part of it.

The gardener comes with the cold.
The tree is marked for cutting down,
He starts to dig the garden up,
then stops, takes stock, and looks around

notes the state of things and shrugs.
Soon not one leaf of that bare tree
is left to hide what is to come,
to save the couple's modesty.

Cold Weather

When friends or neighbours call around I'm sure
to find something behind dad's wardrobe door
that fits them fine.

Item by item they leave with what survives
of him, of the same size, so many lives
waiting in line.

How many fathers bidding a last goodbye?
He's there in everything they take or try.
How cold it is!

He's there, his back turned, in the evening light.
I meet him in the street and recognise him by sight,
each shadow his.

Homeward

We send her out to the summer kitchen.
She comes back. We take her out
into the country. That will be nice for her,
we say and grow sentimental.

We lock her in a distant institution
but she doesn't forget our faces.
She sets out to look for us,
and weeps on the phone in a strange voice.

We love her, of course, of course we do.
She is our crazy grandmother,
our drooling, hydrocephalic child,
the little dog left at our door.

You can't tie the past to a tree.
It will chew through the string, walk out
of the dining room, out into the road
and start chasing cars.

There have been odd moments of
relaxed and intimate silence
but then it squirms, howls, bites the earth
and wants to come home. But where's home?

Dodo

(for Márta Martin)

There it lies on the kitchen floor,
a long-extinct bird's
long, gaping beak
peeking from under the cloth,

We are in another time zone,
wide-open salad tongs!
The terrified dodo in hiding
is not yet ready to leave us.

Which of us is ready for that?
I reach for it under the tablecloth
and grab its beak: and see,
the bird has disappeared.

Listen bird! If you can't fly
it's best that you disappear.
All that is left of your name
is a pile of lettuce feathers.

I stick the bone-coloured narrow
tongs back in the kitchen drawer,
pressing it among ladles, graters,
and wooden-handled meat knives,

but can hear it opening inside.
It's rebelling, blocking the drawer:
I tug at it, meeting staunch resistance.
It's fighting back, digging in.

It thinks it can hide away.
Which of us does not think that?
On Mauritius, on Mars,
under a low-hanging tablecloth?

I reach through the gap, hunt it down,
and bind its open beak with a piece
of elastic from a jam jar. Done!
That's how it ends. Shut up, dodo.

Oven Glove

Pale, pitiful palm,
washed-out oven glove,
belly crushed, wrinkled,
shrunk after long drying.

Bright mauve at the start,
now blotched and faded:
a wizened hand, its skin
patched with liver spots.

I wonder what you want, mother,
you wrinkled, blotchy hand.
There's just one of you, no pair.
You know there was always just one.

Too frail to embrace or to pick up,
I was a hot little saucepan,
sweat-pearled, feverish, and steaming,
but you didn't reach out for me.

Perhaps I should throw it out.
I really should get round to it.
I shouldn't have bothered to wash it.
I don't even know what I hoped for.

After three solid hours
in boiling water, every last
patch of dark soaks away.
How many lives do you need?

What is the correct setting for this?
There are no settings, just the one
for this ever paler, singleton,
this glove, like a human hand.

Any Country in the World

The pollen was swirling, the crematorium wasn't signposted,
the tin roof of the building with its corkscrew chimney
appeared at the end of the concrete path. I recognised it. Someone
was using a cell phone in the yard. The gate was wide open,
I said hello thinking I should leave but a man stopped me
so I asked the way to the office. If it's about your grandmother
you are just in time, he said, it's all ready to go.
I didn't dare ask him what exactly he meant.
In order for her to be legally cremated I had to produce her ID
proving that she was a citizen of Hungary and that she had died.
I put the papers on the table, a woman was fiddling with a typewriter,
the passport opened precisely on the middle fold like a window
in the airless room, on an official stamp declaring that the bearer
was entitled to travel to any country in the world.

It was a hall in any country of the world and I stood
in front of the grey monitor with its gentle hum
and gazed at my grandmother's face, made-up
as if for a journey while her body rolled down the rails,
and she still looked like herself, only her nose seemed
a little bit sharper, apart from which she looked like any dead person,
mottled with jaundice, her throat yellow, simply a body
now released from the prison of this world of vanities
as they slid her away, and suddenly I couldn't look
and is summoned hence to heaven, so they offered me
a seat, saying, do sit down if you would like to stay to the end,
but I had to go, to collect the children from school,
and they were pushing buttons and the electric hum
began, it was one forty-six. I don't believe in
the resurrection of the weather-beaten body.

In the turbine motor of summer, the sky was babbling dry rain,
I kept blinking, the warm wind still blowing outside,
stirring scratchy clouds, bearing them along, sweeping them
centre-stage but it wasn't for her I was weeping,
we hadn't spoken in years, nor for her face, her hands nor
for my pale childhood, but the body, the body alone, just the body
because that's all there was, skin peeling, lilac fingernails, that's all,
because I am a hollow body and I can't bear not loving you,
because every country in the world is an abandoned body
without a home, because the body would never reach home,
and cars were sounding horns, a cyclist swerved round me
so the dust on the skin slowly settles on the heart,
two hours must have passed and I knew she was still burning
as I set off down a road behind the Auchan warehouse
to find the nearest local train.

The Student

Everything rhymes! – I keep repeating,
the world is a fine web of sound,
alert in every single strand,
and your task is to be the spider!

But she's no spider, says her grimace,
thank god, she thinks, she hears no sounds
and hates me for teaching Monday mornings
when she could be sleeping past nine o'clock.

Look round, I say, at all the rhymes,
this buckle here is a figure at prayer,
here is the hand and here the altar.
The poem you seek is always there.

Some can see it. Gaze at the buckle,
and note the cross of the window frame.
(I wonder what they're writing down).
One girl never brings her notebook.

Why is she here? Does she need the credits?
It is her blue eyes I now address.
I tell her each word is a note of music
on the silent score of our existence.

Too much at once. Five minutes left
for the blonde surreptitiously packing.
I imagine her as a tired media worker,
with a full sound file on her mobile phone.

Yesterday, getting in the bath, I tell them,
I spotted a dead cranefly on the floor,
and, on the pavement, an umbrella inside out,
a belated rhyme: both dead and drenched.

She doesn't get it. I know she doesn't.
But in the break she comes to me
and I give her the register to sign.
We've finished with spiders for today.

She says she was waiting to tell me that
she too has glimpsed strands of the web
but life is simpler. That it is we
who complicate it with talk of rhyme.

She gathers her stuff but stumbles over
her scarf and from her library copy
of *Fatelessness* there slips a slip
of paper, her old lottery ticket.

Rainy Summer

I'm haunted by a sentence, a span into which wordless words are cast,
    the negative of sign and silence, of all sentences the sum and very last,
I sleep ever more deeply, I tap my way, the rest is vacancy,
    it sieves rain into one explosive formula, like relativity,
A very long sentence, so long it stretches as far as Creation,
    so bottomless and vast that I myself can't grasp its operation,
the first most secret part of it lives next to the gas meter in the cupboard
    while the yarn in the closed box tangles itself into a code,
a sentence that contains your eyes and the figure of my son,
    a winding blue river, sparkling with voices, on its seaward run,
that pulls me in like a glittering urn, like a deep cave in the iris,
    one sentence, the sentence that starts, deepens and spirals –

I'm haunted by a sentence, a span into which wordless words are cast,
    a dummy in the heart's ditch, a wing folded and bound fast,
a film that runs homeward, the length of a winding street,
    a windblown mallow skirt on the shores of a tide too fleet,
the sentence talks on when wind dies, and when the rain pours down
    it's the speech behind speech that hides behind grin or frown
sometimes it sounds so near a single word would ensure,
    the crease of a single letter on a sheet that's still naked and pure,
where is that sentence, where, I spend nights burning, awake,
    the sentence out in the wheat fields next to where lightnings break,
it's there somewhere, I sense it, soaking beyond the dyke
    but it's not the one I'm seeking, only something like –

a sentence keeps throbbing, a long scar without memory,
    it pulses under the smooth skin of dreams, that says, wake up, hurry,
a sentence that haunts me, like a wordless, continuous dull pain
    that travels every part of my body and will do so time and again,
one that is constant, unwilling to stand still, to fade, or start here,

a voiceless sentence, one that no one will ever utter or hear,
a sentence that clatters, while the heart tolls in the dark
    like the noise you get in a pebbled courtyard where dogs bark,
it pulses like the sea inside the split hull of a wreck,
    get up, get up, in the slippery coves of a dream it goes, tick, tick.
a call without shore, a whirlpool, drifting to blind waters,
    the sea tugged on moon-strings that a slow drum batters,

a sentence rushes on, a long rhythmic unit without words
    you hear it puffing, an inner voice, as you hurry onwards,
when you stop it falls silent while babbling on in your chest
    it runs and runs perpetually, night and day, without rest,
it's there at the bottom of the whirlpool, in love it's a constant drum
    incapable of speech among chatter, a body forever dumb,
the sentence keeps dancing on limbs that are perfectly dead,
    it suffocates your throat and bawls inside your head,
it gallops up the stairs, eyes closed, to an upper floor,
    it scrambles up mountains, breathless, feverish and sore,
it soars like a rocket, sent blasting into the storm,
    a dead jockey on a sweating black horse heading home,

a sentence slipping past, down the motorway at night
    cuts through the heart, through fog, misses the exit sign,
a sentence, the sound of which throbs through sleet, through thunder-
                                                flash and blight
    whirring past blue headlamps and yes, it's fine, it's fine,
a sentence goes rolling on, its tired eyes closed on the bend,
    that is rolling down the hill but still can't come to an end,
a sentence late to arrive on its icy treacherous way
    that passes the barrier, beyond the beyond, and away,
that thrums in the fog as its catatonic wipers toil,
    past a deserted service station, with light on pools of oil,
a sentence that continues on, navigating by feel,
    that rolls on and on, no hands on the steering wheel,

a sentence is speaking, a silent casting mould,
    a bottomless pool, mere thought, washed down, uncontrolled,
a sentence lapping like waves so you hear nothing else
    this sound not the next, a cloudburst, deaf to the pulse,
a sentence that hums down wires and lurks like a brain within,
    that glides like deep sea currents through a dolphin's skin,
a tattooed sentence, the soundscape of promises not kept,
    that I'd tracked all the way, losing the words I had,
a sentence that contained you, gone yet here, some of each,
    tongue of flame, earth-tongue, speech that knows no speech,
the bodiless body of language, a hidden, hopeless wish,
    embedded in loam-like hush in a bright security dish.